Lucida Handwriting Calligraphy Alphabet Practice Book

Alin Chirita with KD

ISBN: 9798415481729

DEDICATION

Through this material you can practice handwriting with the help of Lucida font, one of the most realistic in the MS Word package. The book is intended both for those who want to improve their handwriting and for initiating the little ones who are just starting out. The little ones can also learn the English alphabet.
I put three example words in each letter that can be written on the right. They are written in the same font.

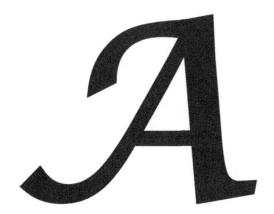

Apple/Alligator/Airplane

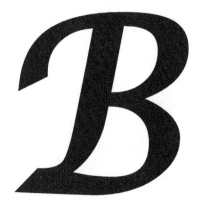

Ball/Banana/Butterfly

Cat/Cake/Castle

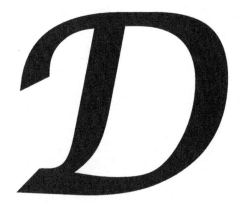

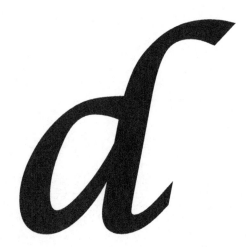

Duck/Dots/Doll

Elephant/Egg/Ear

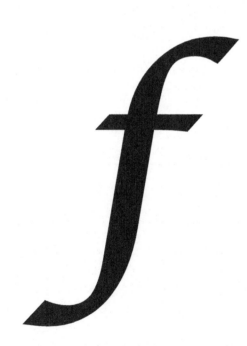

Fish/Flower/Family

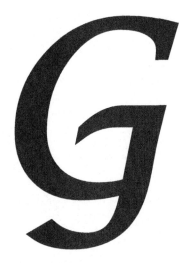

Girl/Green/Grass

House/Horse/Heart

Ink/Insect/Ice

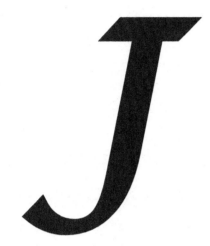

Jelly/Jar/Jaguar

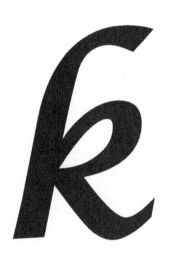

Key/Kangaroo/King

Lion/Leaf/Lips

Monkey/Moon/Mother

Nest/Nurse/Nose

Oven/Onion/Owl

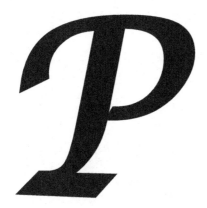

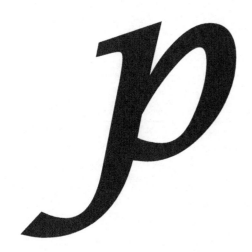

Parrot/Plant/Pan

Queen/Question/Quiet

Calligraphy Practice Book

37

Rabbit/Rose/Robot

S

S

Sun/Sheep/Ship

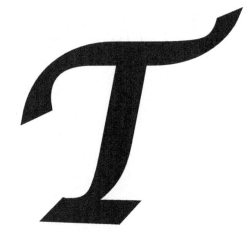

Tomato/Tree/Table

Uniform/Unicorn/Umbrella

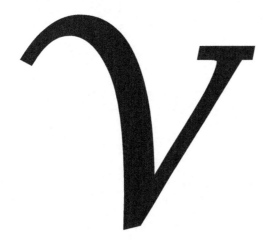

Vase/Vegetable/Vulture

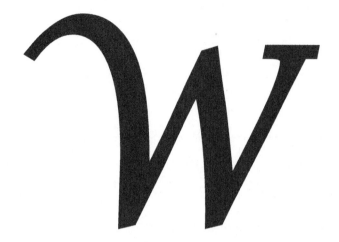

Window/Water/Wall

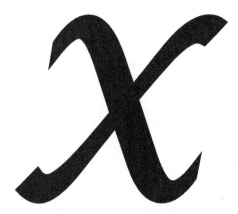

Xavier/X-ray/Xenon

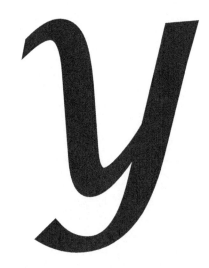

Yellow/Yoga/Yacht

Zebra/Zip/Zoo

ABOUT THE AUTHOR

My name is Alin Chirita and I discovered this service offered by Amazon with which I express my ideas that I hope will be useful for you. I dedicate some of my free time to being creative and I want you to like what I achieve and to be appreciated over time.

Printed in Great Britain
by Amazon

27117874R00033